God Gave Me You

God's Design for your Marriage

By Dan Dooley

Cover Art by Dan Dooley

Published by Dan Dooley at Draft2Digital

All Scripture quotations were taken from New King James Version (NKJV), The New International Version (NIV), or The Living Bible (TLB)

Copyright © 2023 Dan Dooley. All rights reserved.

No part of this publication may be reproduced, distributed, or transmitted in any form or by any means, including photocopying, recording, or by electronic or mechanical methods, or by any information storage or retrieval system without the prior written permission of the publisher, except in the case of very brief quotations embodied in critical reviews and certain other noncommercial uses permitted by copyright law.

Ben Franklin advised: "Keep thy eyes wide open before marriage, and half shut afterwards"

Contents

God Gave Me You i

Introduction v

Chapter 1 - What Is Marriage All About? 1

Chapter 2 - Leaving and Cleaving 5

Chapter 3 - The Question of Compatibility 13

Chapter 4 - Roles 19

Chapter 5 - What is a Home? 29

Chapter 6 - Obstacles to Overcome 35

Chapter 7 - Additional Thoughts 67

From the Author 81

About the Author 83

Other Titles by the Author 84

Introduction

A friend of mine recently told me his definition of love. *"Love is when she asks you to pull on her big toe after she's come home from a hard day of work on her feet. And you do it anyway."*

As humorous and perhaps as distasteful as that story may appear on the surface, when you marry, you are taking on the life and the body of another human being.

Story book ideals aside, her feet are not going to be so pleasant to be near after a hard day of being cramped up in shoes. Are you going to have a moment's hesitation before sacrificing your comfort for hers? That's what marriage is about.

The first addition of this book was written in 2006. At the time, I intended to complete it and publish it. Life and other obligations got in the way, and the project got set aside. And pretty much forgotten.

A lot has changed for me since 2006. My career working years came to a conclusion with my entering into retirement. Life took a horrible turn for me in 2016 when my wife of fifty years was diagnosed with terminal cancer.

The words we had spoken at the altar, as we stood before our pastor, her family, my family and a host of friends and witnesses, became all too real. "Till death does part us."

Every bride and groom should know that, if the marriage lasts that long, that promise is going to be collected sooner or later. As newlyweds, we speak the words because they are part of the ceremony. We give little thought to the reality of it happening to us. After all, we're young - I was twenty-one, and she was twenty - and we're going to live forever. The old "and they lived happily ever after" thing.

Life changes, and with her passing, it changed drastically for me. Nothing was the same. And it has not been the same ever since.

But, if we allow it, there is hope for love after loss. I made the choice. I had been a husband for fifty years. I knew of no reason why I should not continue wanting to be a husband.

God was gracious to me. He sent a wonderful widow my way. Her name is Patsy. Throughout this book, I will make references to her. And to us. We were married in 2018.

Life is certainly different from what it was before. For both of us. But, our life has been blessed greatly. She and I have found opportunities for service, both within the widowed community and within other areas of ministry.

Right now, we are serving in a church which has an emphasis on ministering to the addiction recovery community. That's a new area for us, for it is not within our own personal history, other than experiences with certain family members in the past. But, it is where God has placed us during this season in our lives.

Recently, I remembered this book. Patsy and I have been involved in marriage mentoring and in some sessions with couples struggling with their marriages, many of the points raised in the book have inspired me to spend some time updating the manuscript and preparing it for publication.

Since the time of my wedding with Patsy, I have entered another venture. That of being a published novelist. Thus all the more reason for seeing this book through to completion and publication.

I hope, for the reader, whether couples just beginning, or about to begin their entry into marriage, or pastors and others who use the material presented here for pre-marital counseling, or even an aged couple joining hands in a second, or perhaps even a third or more marriage, that something written here will be words of encouragement and help.

Thanks to my wonderful wife Patsy for proofreading and offering her input, advice, and support on this project.

Chapter 1- What Is Marriage All About?

God Designed Marriage to Satisfy Needs:

Man needed a companion. Humans have a social nature that craves companionship. People naturally crave meaningful relationships. God in His infinite wisdom knew this from the very beginning.

> ***And the LORD God said, "It is not good that man should be alone; I will make him a helper comparable to him."*** (Gen 2:18-19 NKJV)

We need a companion for fellowship and communication. Communication is important, and is a built-in need of every person. We desire someone to talk to. Someone to share hopes, dreams, joys and yes, even sorrows with.

Man needs a completer. God used the term "helper" when he created the companion for man. A companion to provide fellowship, sure, but more than that.

Another human specifically designed by nature to provide assistance, to help him, and to make up those parts of him which make him whole.

That other human being would be like him, but yet unlike him. Opposite, in many ways, both physically and emotionally. Opposite but complementary.

It is no accident of wording that God said, *"they will become one flesh."* The two joined together make a whole. Parts were missing and this was not a defect of creation on God's part.

He intended it to be such. The woman is what is missing in the man, and the man is what is missing in the woman.

The differences in temperament and interests between them are complemented by the addition of the other. In many ways they are opposites, and in nature, opposites do indeed attract.

A good wife will fill in his weak spots. A good husband will let her fill those weak spots.

The reverse is equally true as it applies to the woman.

Men And Women Are Not the Same

Man	Woman
• Achiever	• Helper
• Work Oriented	• Home Oriented
• More Independent	• More Dependent
• Provides for Children	• Produces Children
• More Rational	• More Emotional

Or as the French say, *"Vive la Difference!"* and we men say, "Amen to that!"

Some will object to that division pointing out the differences. In some areas, there will be some overlap of characteristics. Either one can be by nature an achiever. Or work oriented. Or more independent. Or more rational, or more emotional.

Women have become more independent as society and the culture changes. And in many cases men have taken on roles which are more, shall we call, "domestic."

The differences between men and women don't always fall into rigid descriptions. There is a degree of crossover at times. Some women may be higher achievers than their male counterparts for example.

Some women may be less dependent and more work oriented. Some men may be more emotional and less rational, or more home oriented. In general however, these traits are unique to the genders.

The World seeks to distort the differences between men and women, and to even go as far as to remove the differences.

But God's Word defines what a man is, and what a woman is. And God's Word defines marriage. That is the source we adhere to. And that source only.

Chapter 2 - Leaving and Cleaving

God's view of marriage is that there is a leaving, and there is a cleaving:

> ***For this reason a man will leave his father and mother and be united to his wife, and they will become one flesh.*** (Gen 2:24 NIV)

The Living Bible phrases it like this:

> ***A husband and wife are joined together in such a way that "the two become one person."***

Christian marriages are in danger of failing if they do not follow the pattern given in Genesis. If the two partners do not leave their own parents in the broad sense, if they cling to past beliefs, desires and needs, they are not making a clean separation with their pre-married life.

That does not mean they become isolated from family and friends, or interests and activities they enjoyed prior to marriage. But all of those things must take second place now. The marriage takes top priority.

In some cases, where there may have been previous relationships which were either unhealthy, or which would not be suitable for the newly formed marital union, a clean break may be called for.

If there are relationships that you believe to be potentially harmful, they should be sacrificed for the good of your marriage.

A previous marriage, for example. Unless relations have been, and remain good with past marital partners, and relationships, perhaps a clean break may be the wisest choice. You don't want to drag dirty laundry into a brand-new marriage relationship.

Sometimes separation from his or her family presents problems within the new marriage. *It is vital that the two of you identify yourselves as a brand-new family unit separate, and independent from your own parents and the family life you enjoyed while living in your parent's home.*

Serious tensions and strains on the marriage relationship will result if you don't insist on this separation. There is a reason why God did not simply say, "a man will be united with his wife…" but specifically stated that he will leave his father and mother and then be united with his wife.

In past cultures, and this was certainly true of Jewish families at the time of Christ, and even before, family units often did physically live together.

A new groom would bring his new wife into a house unit which had been added to his father's house.

But even with the physical closeness, a distinction, a separation, existed between the new family unit and the rest of the family.

Call it an emotional separation, perhaps, but the new bride and groom now lived together as a new and independent family unit. Husband, wife, and later, children.

Their decisions were their own as well as were their own actions as they pertained to the responsibilities of a husband to his wife and a wife to her husband.

We live in a different time and culture. Now it is less common for newlyweds to literally move in with one of their parents.

And for my part, I am thankful of that. Even with the love I have for my in-laws, I am thankful that we do not, nor have we in the past lived together.

Try your best not to live next door, or too close to either of your parents. You need a physical separation if you are going to establish your own family as an independent unit.

The extended family relationship is important, but it is unhealthy if it takes precedent over your own nuclear family, or if it blurs the lines between the two units.

The family unit should be, and the term we use is the nuclear family, father, mother and children. Or in another term, husband, wife, and children. That doesn't mean that you must move to the opposite side of the country. Simply set boundaries, and adhere to them.

Wife, for you it may be harder than it is for him. Even so, it is just as vital that you do so. No one is expecting you to break contact with your family, but now your dependence is to be on your husband and not on your father.

Rely on your husband to solve the problems of household and automotive repairs, if he is so capable. Don't call on your father to repair your car if your husband is capable of doing the job. And that applies to any household maintenance task.

Of course, there will be those instances where her father (or his) has skills and expertise which the new husband does not have. Never hesitate to call for help when and where it is needed.

Certainly you will still have need of parental advice from time to time. So will he. The two of you as a couple will often solicit the advice of parents or other family members on matters of importance.

Do it as it is mutually agreed between the two of you. Try to deal with your problems first before resorting to the help of others.

Wife, chances are, you have an intimate relationship with your mother deeper than the one he has with his. You share a confidence with your mother, and although it is good, may present problems if you go overboard in revealing things which should remain between you and your husband.

Be careful. There are things to share. And there are things to keep quiet about. *Don't be so quick to criticize him.* He is only human, and he is doing the best he can. Besides, he is learning. He will get better in time if *you* will fulfill your role of helper to him.

Husband, don't dump on your wife to your friends. *Never criticize her to others whether in her presence of not.*

That said, if there are hints of trouble, or there are things going on which pose a real or potential danger to you or your children, then you are within your right, and in fact, you have a responsibility to bring those things to light. Don't keep abuse, whether it is physical, mental or emotional, a secret.

***

I should not have to add this, but it must be said. Husband, don't take out your frustrations on your wife. No matter how much pressure you may be under, whether in your work place, or from any other source, do not act aggressively toward her in any way. Neither physically, nor verbally.

Couples, you must learn this BEFORE the wedding. If there is a tendency toward violent behavior, if there are any hints that one of you is prone to violent reactions, it will not magically get better after you are married. It will be just the opposite. It will get worse.

Though it is demonstrated by men more than by women, women are not immune to violent behavior on their own part.

Wife, do not overlook the red flags. I know you are living in the fog of romanticism. That is part of the idealism we operate under. We want to believe that love is perfect.

It not only solves all of our problems, it provides all we need to have a happy life. But the old saying is, Love is blind. Nevertheless, there is a time to be wide eyed and alert.

Watch out for the warning signs. Do not ignore them. Friends and family members may warn you as well. Learn to be discerning enough to know when they are warning you of real danger, and not simply trying to toss a spanner in the workings of your happiness.

***

You must cleave to your partner in all that this represents. It is no longer a matter of "I". It is now "We". Cleaving implies gluing together. It becomes an inseparable union. You are no longer two. You are one.

Like the weaving of individual threads into a fabric that is stronger by many times the strength of the individual threads, the threads of your two lives are woven together into a union that is stronger than the two individuals.

***

Recently, Patsy and I witnessed a demonstration whereby toilet paper was used to create a rope. Long strings of sheets of common toilet paper were individually wound tightly.

Then three such long wound strings were woven together as cords into a rope form. The result was a rope which was strong enough to withstand the pull of two people, one on each end, without breaking.

***

If something as weak, and flimsy as a string of toilet paper sheets could be made into a strong rope, how much more can the bonding of two people who fully commit to each other, be expected to be? It will be very strong.

> ***Though one may be overpowered by another,***
> ***two can withstand him.***
> ***And a threefold cord is not quickly broken.***
> (Eccl 4:12 NKJV)

Once individual threads are woven together into a fabric, the look of the individual gives way to the look of the whole. Likewise, the strength of the individual gives way to the strength of the whole.

***

We make this claim over our marriage. We are not a marriage of two, but of three. She, me, and God at the head. You should consider doing the same for your marriage.

***

You belong to each other. You are no longer your own.

The Apostle Paul states it this way:

> ***"The wife's body does not belong to her alone but also to her husband. In the same way, the husband's body does not belong to him alone but also to his wife."*** (1 Cor 7:4-5 NIV)

A license, a ceremony, and an exchange of vows do not make a marriage. Living together and consummating it does not create a marriage. A marriage is created and exists upon a cleaving and weaving relationship.

It is the God created and blessed "we" relationship between two people who experience themselves as one, and who act accordingly.

Chapter 3 - The Question of Compatibility

The principle of "right man/right woman" does have biblical backing.

> *And the LORD God said, "It is not good that man should be alone; I will make him a helper comparable to him."* (Gen 2:18-19 NKJV)

And:

> *"Haven't you read," he replied, "that at the beginning the Creator 'made them male and female,' and said, 'For this reason a man will leave his father and mother and be united to his wife, and the two will become one flesh'? So they are no longer two, but one. Therefore what God has joined together, let man not separate."* (Matt 19:4-6 NIV)

I believe that God has a special person for each of us. I don't believe that it is a gamble, or a one in a million chance that we'll be able find that one ideal mate set aside by God for us.

The mate God has set aside for us is not somewhere on the opposite side of the world. God allows our paths to cross. After all, He does control the very rising and setting of the sun.

***

Patsy drove a distance of more than seventy miles to the meet and greet where the two of us met for the first time.

She could have chosen to stay home that evening. Or I, for that matter, could have chosen to stay home that evening.

I did not have that far to drive, but I was new to the widowed fellowship group, and I went there only as the result of an invitation, not knowing a soul there.

a group of total strangers who I had only one thing in common with. We had all lost our spouses.

I believe our meeting, and our resulting marriage was, and is God ordained. You too can gain that feeling about your own meeting and marriage if we allow Him to be the one who has brought you together.

Sometimes that means waiting. Don't settle. You will know early in the dating relationship if you're simply settling.

If you feel like he or she is your only chance, or they are simply the first one to come along, or you don't feel that assurance that he or she is THE one, then you may be settling.

Both Patsy and I had met others following our widowhood. We looked at each one as possible prospects for future marriage.

None were. But when we met each other, both of us knew. We had each been praying for God to send the one of His choosing and He did.

***

Unfortunately, not every believer goes along with God's desire. Mistakes are made, and rebellion on our part can cause us to miss out on God's best for our lives.

And simply put, mistakes happen. In the naivety of youth for example, we don't always use the best judgement.

Mistakes can be made right, and God is more than willing to forgive and allow for fresh starts. He takes us from where we are right now. It is the rest of your life that counts both for Him and for the one God has given us as helpmate.

Some couples, or individual partners within a couple we engage with in marriage mentoring or counseling are on their second or perhaps marriage.

Mistakes almost always result in shame, doubt, and even damage to an individual's sense of self-worth. And, they can create doubts about the hope of success of a new marriage.

"I failed at marriage before. What makes me think this one will fare any better?"

Now how would you answer this question? "Suppose I meet someone and fall in love, and we marry. Then later I meet someone who I find myself loving and I'm convinced that this one was really the right one for me.

"Did I make a mistake with the first one? Perhaps he (or she) was not the right one for me."

I've never had anyone ask that question of me. But I have read and heard of it being asked. I suppose the closest I could come to a meaningful answer is to say that perhaps in this marriage relationship, there is a problem with the idea of commitment.

After all, there is this thing we call "fickleness." That's my thought on the matter, for what it's worth.

But that question is asked all too often. And it is perhaps one of the common causes of divorce. It is not the only cause. But with the prevalence of marital infidelity within our culture, it's not hard to see it happening. The new found love interest will always seem truer to what we want in a marriage.

The newness, the difference, the appearance of what looks like greater beauty, and the sameness of the relationship with the one at home all says, "this one is the right one for me."

Thus the affair begins. And the divorce follows. And if a new marriage results, how long will it be before the one now at home becomes old hat, to use that expression?

When we let God lead, and give Him control of our life, we must begin to trust Him to guide our steps. That does not mean that there will not be challenges, even points of doubt that the marriage will survive the storms.

But keeping focused on the One who makes all things right, our chances of success are greatly multiplied.

Experiencing a failed marriage in the past does not mean your new marriage is doomed to fail. But it is important to have learned the lessons the failed marriage, or marriages taught.

Those things do teach lessons. If we're willing to learn from those lessons, we're better off the next time around.

Stay in God's will, and the rest of your life will be fulfilled. Your life together as a couple will be blessed by Him if He is allowed to be the center of your lives and your home.

True compatibility consists of mutual tolerance, virtue, love, your personal love for God, your unconditional love for your spouse, and your occupation with Christ.

> *So Boaz took Ruth and she became his wife.*
> *Then he went to her, and the Lord enabled her*
> *to conceive, and she gave birth to a son.*
> (Ruth 4:13-14 NIV)

You are tolerant of each other's faults and imperfections. You are motivated to love by the virtues you see in each other. *You also hold an unconditional love for each other, for even when the expectations of the other's virtues are not met, you still love.*

That is, in the early infatuation stage, love is blind, and you see only the good in your mate but never the bad, you are loving based on the *good*.

With the passage of time, your eyes are opened to the not so good. The smelly feet, the irritating little quirks, and the differences of likes or dislikes perhaps, you still love.

You love without conditional considerations. You love because you love and you need no other motivation.

That is a perfect example of the love of God for us. He loves us in spite of our weaknesses and our un-loveliness.

You are attracted, and you form a bond when you become united in spirit, outlook, principles, and mutual interests and likes. You enjoy the company of him or her for reasons that go beyond the basic physical attraction to the opposite sex.

You will find that you have so many interests in common. You'll both enjoy the same things. Not completely of course, as you are two unique people and you will have your unique interests, and opinions.

In the main though, your values and principles and outlook on life will be, or should be aligned.

A couple does not have to share all common likes and interests to be compatible. Compatibility is not about both of you liking the same things. Or even hating the same things.

Certainly it helps if both of you share the same values and standards. It at the least, makes life smoother and it will result in less conflict. Especially if one or both of you are prone to be shall we say, opinionated.

And by all means, that should include spiritual matters. The Bible is clear on the admonishment to be "equally yoked together."

Should both of you be committed Christians before you even think about marriage? I will just say, it will go better for you and your marriage if you are.

Chapter 4 - Roles

That there are roles in marriage is something few new couples want to think about. Or talk about. Or admit that there are roles for each person in the marriage.

Whose job will it be to pay the bills each month? What about making coffee every morning before work? There is also the nasty rubbish bin bag in the kitchen closet to take out when it fills. Never mind rolling the dumpster out to the curb on trash pickup day.

Somebody has to do it. Which of you will it be?

***

The first argument - or was it just a serious discussion? - my late wife and I had following our wedding those many years ago, involved the question; who's going to mind the check book?

Meaning, who would be the one to write the checks to pay bills, make payments, and to keep the book in order.

For some reason which I have long forgotten, I thought it should be my role. But she thought it should be her role.

However the question ended up getting discussed, and the decision arrived at, I do not remember. But she won. And it did not take me long to realize how grateful I was that she won that one.

Not that I could not have managed it, I think I could have. But she was so much better at it. She had a head for such things. Much more so than I did. Or even do today.

***

The small details aside, there are natural roles each person in the marriage will fill. These are roles defined in God's Word. They are outlined in the Scripture passages below.

Outside of those, it will be up to the two of you to determine what your day-to-day roles are, and what will be the major, as well as the minor roles within the marriage.

1. Role of the Husband

> ***Husbands, love your wives, just as Christ loved the church and gave himself up for her to make her holy, cleansing her by the washing with water through the word, and to present her to himself as a radiant church, without stain or wrinkle or any other blemish, but holy and blameless. In this same way, husbands ought to love their wives as their own bodies. He who loves his wife loves himself.***
> (Eph 5:25-29 NIV)

The love Christ commanded the husband to have for his wife is representative of the love of Christ for the church. It is total and unconditional. It is protective and it is sacrificial.

Christ gave His life for the Church, and your love for your wife should be so unconditional and *her* directed that you would be willing to sacrifice your own life for her.

God made the man to be the authority figure in the marriage. That role was established in the garden of Eden.

That is not a master/slave sort of authority relationship. She is a "princess" to be cared for, protected, and provided for.

It is a helping relationship, and her inputs and contribution to the management of the home and family is to be valued and respected. In any relationship, one will have to hold the position of the final word or authority.

Your role is to love her. To choose to love her is fulfilling your role in the relationship. Christ loves the Church with no regard to her returning His love.

He loves her with no regard to her worthiness of His love. That is perhaps more than most men can achieve but I believe that a husband should strive for that level of love for his wife.

That means it is going to be hard at times. Your heart is going to be broken at times. Stop and think though how God's heart is broken when we as His Church fail in our love and our submission to Him.

2. Role of the Wife

> ***Wives, submit to your husbands as to the Lord. For the husband is the head of the wife as Christ is the head of the church, his body, of which he is the Savior. Now as the church submits to Christ, so also wives should submit to their husbands in everything.***
> (Eph 5:22-24 NIV)

Submission does not mean that she is in any way inferior, or that she holds an inferior position to the man.

The functions of a man and woman are different, but the essence is the same. Both are held in equal value by God.

The word "submission" causes many problems today. It actually means "to put ourselves under the leadership of…" That same directive applies to all believers. We submit, or put ourselves under the leadership or authority of Christ.

The wife is not a slave to her husband. She is not a stepping stone to be walked on, disrespected, or abused in any way, mentally, emotionally, spiritually, or physically. She is to be your partner. Your helper. Your confident. Your lover. Your best friend.

She is to be valued above all you have. And more than anyone else in your life. She is to be honored.

It is interesting that the passages related to the roles of the husband and the wife never say that the wife is commanded to love her husband as it commands the husband to love his wife.

I don't believe the admonition was any intent to eliminate the suggestion that love would exist in the heart of a wife for her husband. I think it was a simple assumption needing no statement.

If the husband does his part, and lives his role as God intended, and the wife is committed to living her own life obedient to the Will of God, that love is going to be a natural result.

As we are expected to love Christ, the wife is expected to love her husband. That is, Christ wants us to and hopes we will love Him. Likewise, the husband wants his wife to love him.

The question of "choice" returns to be examined. If there is one thing God cannot do, or perhaps I should say "will not do" is make us love Him.

He could, but He made the choice not to do that. He wants us to love Him on our own, with no magic tricks or coercion on His part.

The husband is commanded to love his wife for in that way he is emulating the role of Christ to the Church. Christ does love the church and if the man is going to fulfill his role faithfully, he must love his wife.

The wife being representative of the Church is not commanded to love her husband any more than the Church is commanded to love Christ. It is expected, and hoped that she will.

It is a special treat when the Church of her choice, with no prompting, no commanding and no coercion, falls in love with Jesus.

From the human side, it is a special thing when the wife of her own choice loves her husband. A real man would want it no other way.

3. Role of God in Your Home

> *"But as for me and my household, we will serve the LORD."* (Josh 24:15 NIV)

The Christian marriage stands as a symbol of the relationship between Christ and the Church. As such, the relationship must include Christ if it is going to function as it should, and as God intended it to function.

The old commercial saying "things go better with Coke" can be paraphrased to say, "married life goes better with Christ."

Christ should be the center of your home life. That means that in all you do, consider Him a vital part of your decision-making process.

And during times of gladness, and in times of sorrow, keep Him in remembrance. Praise Him when times are rough, and praise Him when times are blessed.

Do not neglect prayer time together. Private prayer time is good for you individually and should be a regular part of your daily life. But prayer time which includes both of you will be a source of spiritual strength for the family unit as a whole.

This is especially good when children are included. You are not only uniting your own two hearts in agreement in your love for God, but you are also teaching your children the value of prayer.

***

Our second date ended with prayer. It was a spontaneous thing. As Patsy and I spent some time sitting in her car following our seeing a movie together, we talked.

And the more we talked, the more we each began to feel that where we were going was God ordained and directed.

We had already known that for each of us, God had the right person to fulfil that need each of us had. She desired to have someone to spend the rest of her life with. And so did I.

Now we began to feel that we were that for each other. We began to feel that God was placing us together. But we wanted to be sure.

We prayed together while sitting in her car, seeking God's guidance, and expressing our desire to operate within His will.

By the time I drove back to my home, I was convinced. God had answered my prayer for a godly marriage partner.

That was when we made the decision, that from that night on, we would end each evening with prayer together. If we were physically together, we would pray together in person.

If we were not together, as our last phone call of the evening, we would pray together over the telephone.

That practice continues to this day. We have added the reading of a couple's devotional to our prayer time, but praying together is now a constant ending of our day.

***

Do not neglect Bible reading and study. There is nothing better than prayerful reading and study of God's Word to reveal God's will for your lives individually, and for your family as a whole.

Each of you should have your own independent practice of feeding on the Word. If you have not made a habit of it, now is a great time to start.

> ***Your word I have hidden in my heart, That I might not sin against You.*** (Ps 119:11 NKJV)

How can we hide His Word, making it a part of our inner being, and in such a secure place that it is a guard against sinning, unless we make a regular diet of feasting upon it?

Some have called it "spiritual food." It is indeed food for the soul. With it, the spiritual body grows - I am using figurative speech - and without it, the spiritual body shrivels from malnutrition.

When your children are old enough to understand, read Bible stories to them. Teach them to love and understand the message of God's Word.

Keep the message simple and age appropriate for them. Involve them in Sunday School and other Christian fellowship appropriate for their age.

Don't neglect corporate fellowship with fellow believers. We strengthen each other. We need each other. We need the fellowship and we need the feeding received through the deliverance of the Word from the pulpit and in Sunday School.

I strongly encourage you, as a couple. If you have not already made a practice of regular church attendance, begin to do so now. Even if you are not yet married. It is a habit which will serve you well throughout your married life.

Find a local church to attend and become a part of. By "local," I mean just that. One that is relatively close to where you live.

One close enough to you geographically to allow you to become a part of the community of that church.

Make friends within the church. Certainly you will have friendships outside of the church setting, but the more you become a part of friendships with other couples within your age level, the more connected you will feel, and actually become.

We need the fellowship of fellow Christians in our life. We grow spiritually by the encouragement we receive from others, as well as the encouragement we can give to others.

Find a church that teaches and believes in the Word of God. It does not matter what denomination you choose, as long as that church holds its beliefs and teachings in line with God's Word.

I challenge you to make a habit of living your lives in a way that will be a positive testimony to the love of Christ living in you.

Guard your home against ungodly and unhealthy influences. The best defense against the intrusion of harmful influences into your home is to stay grounded in the Word of God and keeping your prayer life healthy.

Elsewhere in this book I give the warning against letting yourself, either individually, or as a couple, into morally compromising activities.

You have been joined together as the Scripture says, "one flesh." Don't let temptations steer you into relationships which are not appropriate for you to be in.

That includes potentially inappropriate friendships with members of the opposite sex. They may seem innocent but there is a real danger of developing into emotional attractions, which can lead to physical attractions and more.

> ***Above all else, guard your heart, for it is the wellspring of life.*** (Prov 4:23 NIV)

And certainly, avoid the trap pornography will drag you into. More on that later in this book.

Chapter 5 - What is a Home?

It is a place where....

Let the Lord be the center of your home and family life.

...Christ Reigns Supremely

***

Although the saying is not of our own invention, Patsy and I often in our prayers, and certainly in our thoughts concerning our marriage, we say, "it is a marriage of three. God, and each of us."

This is one instance in which the old saying, "two is company, three is a crowd" does not apply. If God does not reign at the head of our home, our home is not complete.

***

Unless the LORD builds the house, its builders labor in vain. (Ps 127:1 NIV)

"But as for me and my household, we will serve the LORD." (Josh 24:15 NIV)

...Family Unity is the Norm

There is unity with common faith, convictions, goals, and love.

For a time, your home will consist of just the two of you. The idea of "home" usually conjures up the image of multiple people, more than two. But it begins with just the two of you.

That will change for most couples. Sooner or later children will come along. Or, in some cases, they will not.

Not every home will include children. Some, by choice and some owing to circumstances beyond the control of the couple.

The Family Unit may be father, mother and the kids. Or it may simply be husband and wife.

There may come a time when the family unit changes. Sometimes an elderly parent may be brought into the home. Or another relative, for whatever reason, may move in.

Although we don't want to talk about it, or even to think about it, there will come a time, and it may be sooner than we ever think can happen, one of the partners in a marriage may be taken in death leaving the home no longer feeling like a home.

It is a guaranteed fact of life. Baring a disaster which takes both partners in a marriage at the same time, or the calling away of the saints at that time known only to God Himself, the marriage is going to end. The words spoken at the wedding altar "till death does us part," will be fulfilled.

No new bride and groom ever gives thought to the reality of that wedding promise. After all, they are just beginning life together, and it is supposed to be for "happily ever after."

Likewise, and it is an equal tragedy, sometimes the home is broken as the result of the dissolution of the marriage through divorce.

That is certainly not what the new bride and groom envision while they stand at the altar. And it is not God's desire for their married life. But it happens.

> *Do two walk together unless they have agreed to do so?* (Amos 3:3 NIV)

...You Find Refuge and Quiet

Your home is a shelter from the storms of life and the pressures of society.

Even for those who share the home, just the two of them, home is home. It is, or should at least, be the place of refuge from the hassles and the hustle and bustle of the world outside the front door.

> *It is better to live in the corner of an attic than with a crabby woman in a lovely home.*
> (Prov 21:9 TLB)

***

Thankfully, I do not live in a home with a crabby woman. Patsy is not crabby by nature. Sometimes it's a wonder, living with me. But she's a saint. And I am blessed.

Our home is a place of rest for us. Even in my married years with my late wife, that was always the case.

Now during the child raising years, a home can experience a certain degree of chaos. And stress. That's just part of the process during those years.

Throughout my career years, I traveled extensively. I spent many nights in hotels. I ate by myself in restaurants. I spent many hours seated in an airliner.

But with each trip, there came that leg of travel which brought me back to my home airport and then to home.

Walking in the front door, I was home. And no matter how hectic the previous few, or several days had been, I could kick off my shoes, and enjoy what was now my sanctuary.

Even in the earlier years when the boys were young, and not always so quiet, the sense of peace and relaxation I felt helped put the stresses of work life aside.

Not that there was never some stress and noise. A home is not a mortuary. Living people live there.

There will be some degree of bustle, of noise, and even now and then some tension. Perhaps even strife. What do you expect when real people are involved?

***

…Spiritual Growth Thrives

A place for your personal quiet time, and for your family devotions, prayer and study of the Word.

> ***I will walk in my house with blameless heart. I will set before my eyes no vile thing.***
> (Ps 101:2-3 NIV)

Home is that place where it all begins for the children you will, or will hope to bring into the marriage.

Not only is home the place where the two of you will spend time in prayer and sharing devotions together, it should be the place where Bible stories are read to the kids and bedtime prayers are made each night.

Sunday morning, listening to the pastor and the Sunday School teacher expound on the Word of God is not enough. We need a time at home to spend reading God's Word, and growing from the experience. And prayer time. Individually and even privately. And, for your time as a couple.

This is how spiritual growth comes about. The environment where study and meditation on the Word occurs best is that place where calm and quiet are most felt.

Chapter 6 - Obstacles to Overcome

Getting married and setting up housekeeping, beginning a life together, is not like children playing the game "house." Or "playing house" as they call it.

It is suddenly real life and it is filled with adult reality. It sounds fun before it begins, and really, it can be the makings of fun, but it is also frightening.

The issues a couple faces, almost from day one; or at least after the formal honeymoon is over, can quickly become overwhelming.

1. Finances/Budgeting

Decide who is going to be responsible for the task of keeping the finances in order. It may be both of you, but chances are one of you will be better suited for such detail work.

Don't be rigid about it. As in, "it's his or her job to keep the checkbook in order. I'm not going to do it." Make sure that the one doing it is actually going to be fiscally responsible.

More arguments are held over family finances than just about any issue within a marriage. If your family finances are in a mess, most other areas within your family life will be as well. Spend well, but spend carefully.

There is no harm in enjoying the nice things of life. Just make sure you can afford them. Be careful with the use of credit and credit cards. They're convenient but they can lead to trouble if not used responsibly. Create and follow a responsible budget.

Practice good stewardship with your finances as though the money belongs solely to God, and you are just using it for now.

Don't be stingy with your money. Be always aware of the needs of others. After all, the saying that *"it is more blessed to give than to receive"* (Acts 20:35) is true.

Not only will you bless others by your giving, you are making an investment in the lives of others for now and eternity. The Bible says, **"God loves a cheerful giver."** (2 Cor. 9:7)

The Bible speaks much on the subject of giving, and it will bless your lives as well. And don't forget God's share. When God blesses you financially, honor Him in return with your giving.

Don't limit that giving to money alone. Your time, talents and abilities as well as your praise and worship are owed to Him.

Through all of that though, do not neglect the financial and material needs of your own family. Be generous with your resources, talents and abilities, but be responsible.

Being generous does not mean being irresponsible. There is giving for good cause, and there is giving for other than good cause.

Make sure to use good wisdom when choosing where and to whom to give. Don't throw away your money on bad causes.

***

"Who's going to pay for the movie tickets tonight?

Shortly after Patsy and I began going together, we faced an interesting situation, which seemed normal for us, but may not be for other couples.

Perhaps because we knew that we were going to be together for good, and it was not going to be a short-term thing. And perhaps it was because for us, it was not our first trip around the block.

We did not approach anything in life the same way we did when we were much younger and entering marriage for the first time.

Initially, I paid for movie tickets. I paid the restaurant bills. I paid for any activity we participated in. And that's the way it usually is in a dating relationship. At least in the beginning.

But times are not as they were when we each began dating in our youth. For me, that now being closer to sixty years ago. Couples often share expenses now. At least for those of us in later years with other marriages behind us.

So sometimes I paid for the evening. And sometimes she did. But we were already feeling like a married couple in some ways, and this alternating of paying seemed, well, tiring.

We decided that even though we were not yet married - and no, we were not living in ways which would not be pleasing to God - we opened a joint bank account and obtained debit/credit cards on that account.

Each of us with one in our own name. And we each deposited an equal amount of money.

From that bank account we paid for our dating activities.

We, for some time, retained our individual bank accounts which we had had before we met. But soon, everything came out of that one account, and in time, it became our only account.

We have long since deactivated any other bank accounts, and now we have just one. The one we set up early in our dating days.

What we did is not a practice I would advise every yet to be married couple to do. Especially, a young couple still uncertain of what the future holds for them. We knew what the future held for us. But remember, we were not novices at life and marriage.

***

For young couples just beginning their adult life out on their own, away from their parents' homes, one of the first steps in financial management usually means opening up a bank account. Typically with a debit or debit/credit card.

All of their mutual expenses, including those expected for their household will be paid from that account.

If they are both working, very likely they will have their employment pay deposited into that account.

But, if the two, or even one of the two has been on their own for a time before the marriage, that one likely already has a banking relationship.

For couples entering marriage later in life, perhaps following widowhood or divorce, it is almost assured that they will enter the marriage with their own individual banking relationships.

It will be up to the individual couple to decide how their finances and banking accounts will be managed. Will they retain individual bank accounts.

Often these accounts are maintained for the convenience of spending which is for the individual rather than for the joint financial transactions of the couple.

Some have elected to use their individual accounts and divide their contribution for the household needs. For example, they may agree that out of his income the house and car payments are paid. Out of her income, the groceries and utilities are paid.

Personally, I am of the opinion that common use obligations should be mutually shared. For that reason, I would urge couples, even if they desire to retain separate banking accounts for their own individual use, to have a common account equally managed between them.

Each to contribute into that common account out of their source of income. Thus all bills including car and house payments (or rent), groceries, utilities, and even entertainment, come out of that common account.

Why? We have seen financial strife result when one or both begin the feel that there is inequity in contributing to the needs of the household. This is especially common when other stresses are present within the marriage.

"I pay all of the mortgage, the insurance and even the car payments. She does not keep up her end. Sometimes I even have to pay the grocery bills. And the cable. She pays the other utilities. That's all she contributes."

Do you see the problem? That should be the last thing any couple should be arguing over. It could be so much easier and avoid being a point of contention, if that part of the financial picture was shared all in common.

2. Household Duties/Chores/Responsibilities

> ***The LORD God said, "It is not good for the man to be alone. I will make a helper suitable for him."*** (Gen 2:18 NIV)

God did not create the woman to be the slave of the man. She was created to be his helper. That has to presume that as she is his helper, he too must be her helper.

Don't be afraid to share chores and duties around the house. It should never be a "his jobs and "her jobs". Husband, you may be tired from a day's work but so is she.

Likewise, when he is tired, and perhaps has had a very rough go of it at work, is that honeydo project really necessary right now? Can it wait until later?

Some things, of course, should not wait. Others certainly can and probably should. Be wise enough to know the difference. If the bathtub is overflowing because of a stopped-up drain, now is the time to deal with it.

If she suddenly has the urge to repaint the hall bathroom, perhaps a better planning of the time to do it would be helpful.

Do things together and share tasks as much as possible. Husband, help her out when you can. Wife, help him out when you can.

You're each going to have your particular skills, talents and interests. One will be better at home repairs. One will be better at cooking.

Consider those and like tasks your individual roles. Both are necessary to the efficient maintenance of the household. Both are equal in honor within the home.

Don't consider them mutually exclusive based on your gender and assumed roles. Wife, you may have occasion to help him in a repair project.

Husband, she may ask you to chop onions, or stir a cake batter for a while, when her arm grows tired. Don't make her carry out the trash though. That job is uniquely ours. Well, it should be. But you get my point.

3. Intimacy/The Sexual Part of Marriage/Loving

God created marital intimacy for pleasure. Sure, the act of sex is for the procreation of the human race but it is equally if not more so, for your mutual pleasure and emotional satisfaction.

The Bible is very clear that it is for your pleasure. The command, *"may you rejoice in the wife of your youth."* (Prov 5:18 NIV) cannot be taken in any way other than to say, enjoy her. Have fun with her. Experience physical pleasure with her.

An entire book of the Bible (The Song of Solomon) is devoted almost exclusively to the romantic and physical side of love.

Some might – though it is not so common today – tend to downplay the importance of sex within marriage. Others would make of it something dirty or unwholesome. They are totally wrong to do so. It is extremely important in the relationship.

I will go as far as to say, if the sexual relationship between a couple is not healthy, then the marriage relationship itself is not healthy. It is in danger as well.

It is the healthiest of human interactions and is necessary for emotional, as well as physical health. It is an appetite which must be satisfied.

The Apostle Paul gave instructions for married couples concerning this area. He realized that the need for intimacy is strong and persistent.

> *"Do not deprive each other except by mutual consent and for a time, so that you may devote yourselves to prayer. Then come together again so that Satan will not tempt you because of your lack of self-control."* (1 Cor 7:5-6 NIV)

Even in this supposedly enlightened time, sometimes one partner will for whatever reason deprive the other. Paul charged that this is unhealthy, and it's wrong. It opens up the opportunity for temptations as well as impure thoughts and actions.

> *He who is full loathes honey, but to the hungry even what is bitter tastes sweet.* (Prov 27:7 NIV)

That verse means that when you are filled to satisfaction, no matter how tempting the offer of more may be, it is not attractive. When you are hungry or starved, even the not so attractive, tempts.

Learn to know each other's needs, desires and even limitations. Learn to share your needs with your partner. Learn to be open to your partner.

Hiding secret desires is not healthy. Your partner is not a mind reader. He or she cannot know what you want or need unless you let it be known.

Learn to make adjustments for the needs and desires of your partner. After all, loving is about give and take. It's not all about you. That said, it is also about you. This includes but also goes beyond just the physical or the sexual part of the relationship.

There will be times when one of you may not feel the need that your partner feels. That's normal, but if it's not handled correctly, and in love and with consideration of your partner, resentment and frustration will be the outcome.

It is often said, and a statement could hardly be truer, that "Love is a choice". That means *you choose to love*. You make a willful decision to love.

You are not always going to feel like loving your partner, whether that means the sexual relationship or other expressions of love. Your partner should not make unfair demands on you, nor should you make unfair demands on your partner.

There will be times when due to fatigue, health, or other factors, your physical desires are not the same as your partners. Be understanding of your mate when he or she cannot fulfill your immediate needs.

Ideally those times should be short lived, if not infrequent. If they become the norm rather than the exception, then you really need to examine the cause of the problem, and seek solutions to resolve, or at least lessen the impact upon your relationship.

Sex is not love any more than love is sex. They are, or should be, a part of each other. There is a relationship between the two. They don't have to coexist, but they are more complete, and are in line with God's design if they do.

I contend that you can have sex without having love. I do not believe that you can have whole marital love without sex being a major ingredient.

The Bible never teaches abstinence between married couples with the exception of the brief time allowed in the 1st Corinthians passage quoted above.

There is the matter of *choosing* to love. We are not nor should we be slaves to our hormones. If we can only be intimate when our hormones drive us, then we are being lazy in our relationship.

Our hormone performance can come and go. Our love should not. Our determination to love our mate should not.

That said, the physical body has its limitations. Sometimes the hormones do not work as they should, and that can affect ability. This can affect both men and women, although men will be most affected when it comes to the physical ability part.

Generally, with advancing age, the loss of certain abilities becomes greater. But men of any age are not spared from the possibility of such loss.

Dealing with the problems described above is beyond the scope of this book. There may be cause to seek professional help for persistent and/or long-term problems.

I know I am, as they say, "preaching to the choir" when I discuss these things with a couple eager to begin their marriage, and who cannot wait to start enjoying each other in that special way.

But time often has a tendency to temper the most passionate of emotions and actions. The best thing you can do is to keep the interest and desire going. It can and should last for the rest of your natural lives.

In time it will change, and even the frequency may lessen a bit but it should never go away. Then it will be more important than ever to make the conscious choice to express love to your mate.

If in the beginning of your married life, you have learned to make a habit of choosing to love, it will become second nature for you.

Never be afraid to show affection. Husband, it *is* manly and okay to kiss your wife or hold her hand, or to otherwise touch her. Even in public.

Especially, be sure you are quick and eager to express affection to her before your children. That is the best example you can show to them the way they should act towards their future marriage partners.

Plus, it reaffirms your love and commitment to their mother, and assures them that you intend to stay with her.

It is a sign to them that both parents will remain together. Children are fearful enough of the risk of parental separation. They see friends whose parents are splitting up, and it's easy for them to fear the same of their own parents.

This applies equally to stepchildren. They've already seen one breakup in the family unit, and are fearful that it may happen again.

Besides, you are reaffirming your feelings to your wife. Touch her as often as you can. When you are within arms reach, there should be a touch. She needs it and so do you.

Wife, the same goes for you. He enjoys and needs your touch as much as you enjoy and need his.

This may come as a surprise but no; she has no way of knowing that you love her unless you tell her. I mean verbally.

You may have the greatest sex life, and your time together may be filled with bliss, but she still will not know that you love her unless you say it using those three magic words, "I love you."

Don't respond to her question of, "do you love me?" with the old, "of course, you know I do." That doesn't cut it. Never use the old excuse that you have trouble expressing yourself.

Balderdash! I won't buy that, and you can be assured that she won't either. Learn to say it. And say it often. How often? How many times a day do you eat? By all means, when you say it, mean it.

Doing things for her, though of themselves they are expressions of love, does not prove to her that you love her. Providing for her financial and security needs does not prove that you love her as a woman, and as your lover.

After all, you might do the same things for a close friend, or for your mother. Never just assume that she knows it by what you *do* for her. Or even how well you love her in the physical. You really must speak the words to her.

Wife, here's a news flash for you too. *He has no idea that you love him unless you tell him.* No matter how well you keep the house, cook fantastic meals, provide for his every creature comfort, or how well you raise the kids, or even how well you make physical love to him.

If you never verbally tell him, unprompted, that you love him, he's likely to have doubts that you really do. He certainly will not be completely assured of your love for him.

He may see you as one dependent upon him for emotional, security and or physical needs, but he'll suspect that's all he means to you. True or not, that thought will haunt him. Be aware that *there is a difference between loving someone and being dependent upon someone.*

I am now going to speak on a subject which is almost taboo and is avoided too often to the detriment of many marriages. The plague of pornography.

Every man, at some point in his life, and it often begins in childhood years comes face to face with pornographic images, whether they be somewhere on the Internet, or even within books and magazines.

Women are not immune to the exposure, but it appears that men are the ones most often to become slaves to this evil.

Yes, I called it evil and I said that it is enslaving. Pornography is very much like a drug. It is addicting. You cannot simply take a little and then let it go.

You will want more and in time it will replace the natural affection and desire you should have for your wife.

And, you will want more than just what the early exposures provide. The initial thrill and stimulation grows dull with repetitive exposure. Then more and more explicit material is needed in order to thrill and stimulate.

What the mind now craves is more than your own wife can provide to satisfy your sexual needs. You may even reach the point where you drag her into the same addiction.

I have heard too many even Christian men admit that they have become addicted to pornography. And it's hard for them to break out of the bondage.

***

I will make an admission here. There was a time in years past, even before social media was our normal day to day habitat, that from unknown sources, email messages came into my mailbox which contained links to seductive materials.

Traveling extensively as my career required, nights in hotel rooms became lonely places. And though I was away from my wife at home, my needs and desires as a man continued.

It became tempting to just see what those sites were all about. After all... Well, you get the point.

But I quickly learned that exposure meant that the desire to continue to look grew. I recognized the danger, and what the outcome would be if I allowed myself to continue.

It would have been so easy to simply let myself enjoy the offerings. After all, who was to know? And what harm was I causing?

I knew, and God knew. And as to harm, I could easily find the viewings more stimulating, and more satisfying than my time with my own wife.

I made the decision to cut off any further exposure. The emails when they did come, were immediately deleted. Thankfully, the incoming emails grew fewer and fewer and finally ceased.

Sure, I could continue to search and easily find those sites if I desired. But I decided I was not going to do so.

***

Men, Scripture tells us to guard our hearts and our minds. There are certain places we must not allow ourselves to go if we are to remain true in our marriages.

Lusting after, and being sexually aroused, and even following up on that arousal over images online or in printed material, is simply another form of adultery. It is a way of cheating on your wife. Don't let yourself become caught up in that trap.

4. Children/Born into the Marriage/Brought into the Marriage

> *Like arrows in the hands of a warrior are sons born in one's youth. Blessed is the man whose quiver is full of them. They will not be put to shame when they contend with their enemies in the gate.* (Ps 127:4-5 NIV)

Children born into a marriage are a blessing from God. There is no training manual included. You're almost on your own as to how to raise them. Since they are all unique – no two are alike – there is no formula you can follow with exactness.

Much prayer, study of the Word, and godly support from family and church goes a long way to help. Raising children is an adventure the end of which we in this lifetime may never know.

Come to an understanding between the two of you how many children you would like to have. Decide on an effective and suitable birth control. Decide how soon, or how late you will begin bringing children into the home.

> *Train up a child in the way he should go, and when he is old he will not depart from it.*
> (Prov 22:6 NKJV)

Start early training your children to love God. Make use of Sunday School, Children's Church, Bible stories, and any other means you can to introduce your children to a loving God. Make it fun and easy to understand based on his or her age level.

Consider methods of discipline. Those should be fair and serve to teach rather than punish. It is extremely crucial that *both* father and mother be in complete agreement in all matters of discipline.

The worst thing two parents can do is to oppose each other over an issue in which a child is in the middle. Children are quick to pick up on the possibility that they can play one parent against the other.

Likewise, lack of agreement undermines the authority factor. Be unified. If you have to discuss an area you may disagree over, do it totally out of the presence of the child. When you approach the matter with him or her, be in agreement.

Don't countermand or second-guess your mate. Don't undermine his or her authority. Once that authority has been undermined, it may never be regained in the eyes of the child. Respect for that parent is damaged.

Equally importantly, be consistent in treatment and discipline. Avoid the appearance of favoritism between children. They're all different, and they will have different personalities and present different challenges so this can be tough at times.

You can't treat them all the same though, you should strive to treat them all with equal love, care and attention.

Sometimes children are brought into a marriage from a previous marriage. This situation can be a blessing, or it can be a pure nightmare. How well the situation is made to work is going to depend on how much time, patience, love and prayer are put into the effort.

It is best to discuss possible problems in this area before the marriage. Try to arrive at good decisions and plans ahead of time.

You won't be able to resolve all difficulties beforehand. Some things simply take time and will take care of themselves.

If you are entering a marriage where children are already present, try to become as familiar with, and to the children as you can *before* the marriage. The relationship will continue to grow, and hopefully grow better with time.

There is no reason to wait until his or her kids are completely at ease with you before entering into the marriage. Otherwise, the marriage may never occur.

There may be some resistance on the part of the children of the custodial parent to the entry of a replacement – or so he or she may be viewed – parent into the home.

There may be a secret hope on the part of a child that the missing birth parent may be restored to the family unit.

That child may resent the new husband or new wife as an intruder. Strong emotions may come into play. The two of you will need to deal with these problems and if necessary, professional and godly counseling help may be called for.

Even in the case of the death of a parent, children may resent the entry of a new father or mother into the home. Remember, kids by nature can be selfish.

That's normal and should be dealt with tenderly and with a great deal of patience. Don't rush your marriage if major problems exist in this area. Seek help if needed.

***

As part of the widowed community, Patsy and I have witnessed this first hand. We have seen the resentment of children of a widowed parent against the desires of that parent to find new love after loss.

It is wrong, but it is all too common. Too often children, and this includes adult children selfishly oppose the remarriage of a widowed parent.

It is a point of selfishness. The one who has lost his or her spouse is now alone and loneliness is never a good thing.

We have explained it this way. After the funeral, the family goes home to their own. The widowed goes home to an empty house.

***

The problem of disciplining your mate's children must be settled. The earlier you bring the matter to agreement, the better. The Exact arrangement arrived at will depend on a number of factors.

1. The closeness of the new union.

2. The relationship of the child to his or her non-custodial parent.

3. The acceptance of you into the family by the child.

How much the custodial parent is willing to include you in the disciplining process. Identify and resolve those questions to increase household harmony.

Be active, but don't overstep any boundaries that may be set up within the new family unit, real or perceived.

In time, chances are that you will be more and more perceived as a parental figure. Don't rush it.

5. Acquaintances/His friends/Her Friends

> ***Perfume and incense bring joy to the heart,***
> ***and the pleasantness of one's friend springs***
> ***from his earnest counsel.*** (Prov 27:9 NIV)

Each of you will bring friends and acquaintances into the relationship. Just because they're his friends or her friends, does not mean you will like them, or be able to relate comfortably.

It's great when that happens, but don't be surprised if it doesn't. Likewise, they may not develop a fondness for you.

Friendships often develop to be remarkably strong. Often the bonds between friends are stronger than between family members. Our close friends may be held dearer to us than our siblings, for example.

> ***But Ruth said: "Entreat me not to leave you,***
> ***Or to turn back from following after you;***
> ***For wherever you go, I will go;***
> ***And wherever you lodge, I will lodge;***
> ***Your people shall be my people,***
> ***And your God, my God.***
> ***Where you die, I will die,***
> ***And there will I be buried.***
> ***The LORD do so to me, and more also,***
> ***If anything but death parts you and me."***
> (Ruth 1:16-17 NKJV)

Remember, your mate may have developed his or her friendships over many years and they are valuable and important to him or her. Don't expect that he or she will, just like that, cut off all previous relationships with others.

There may be instances where it is advisable to do so, of course. In the event that he or she has been associated with an unhealthy crowd those ties should be broken. Here though, we're talking about healthy friendships and associations.

Allow your mate time to spend with his or her friends on a social basis. On the other hand, be careful that you are not allowing your friendships to come between you and your new spouse.

The marriage relationship is fragile in its early life and almost anything can spark jealousy. Too many "boys night outs" or "girls night outs" will build up resentment and a feeling of abandonment by your new spouse.

Each of you must be both understanding and flexible. Your first responsibility is to your spouse, above all others. You owe more to your marriage than you do to even lifelong friendships, no matter how close those friendships.

Retain those relationships, but be sure that all parties know your spouse has first claim to your time and your attention.

The best thing you both can do is to form, if they don't already exist, are mutual friendships. Other couples you both enjoy a friendship with.

6. The Extended Family

> *I will drive him like a peg into a firm place; he will be a seat of honor for the house of his father. All the glory of his family will hang on*

> *him: its offspring and offshoots--all its lesser vessels, from the bowls to all the jars.*
> (Isa 22:23-24 NIV)

When you marry someone, you are in a very real sense joining another family. You become a part of your mate's family. Ideally, you will accept them as your new family, and they will accept you as an important part of their family. Ideally, you will like and even grow to love each other.

Now that you have two families, how are you going to divide your time of visits and attention between them? Expect that there may be tensions and perhaps even arguments between you and your mate over the question of where you are going to spend holidays. Here again, flexibility on the part of both of you will be very important.

Husband, expect that your wife is going to favor her family over your family, especially at holiday times. She will feel much stronger about being with her family than you will about being with your family.

She will want to visit them more often than she will want to visit yours. There are exceptions but this is the more common fact.

Wife, be understanding of your husband. He loves his family as much as you love yours. It is normal for men to release themselves from their families more readily than women from their families.

That does not mean he wants to leave them out of the picture completely. He may very well give in to your preferences for spending holidays with your family but if that is carried too far, he will be resentful of it.

Come to a good compromise between you. Due to geographic distances, it may be easier to spend holidays with one family rather than the other. That may simplify the matter, at least on the surface. If possible, try to share visiting time.

If both families are close by, come to a mutual agreement as to how you will split your time between them. Even on the same day it should be possible to visit both families.

Don't let what should otherwise be joyous holiday seasons become a point of contention between you and your mate.

7. Careers/His job/Her job

> *Do you see a man skilled in his work? He will serve before kings; he will not serve before obscure men.* (Prov 22:29 NIV)

> *You will eat the fruit of your labor; blessings and prosperity will be yours.* (Ps 128:2 NIV)

Traditionally the man has been the breadwinner in the family. Even more traditionally, the man was the one who worked outside the home while the wife remained at home and raised the children.

Now those roles are not so clear-cut. In some cases, the wife may earn a higher income than the husband. And sometimes, the husband may be the stay at home keeper of the fold.

Often major decisions will need to be made related to his or her job or career. What demands will be placed on the family if for example, her job requires her to travel frequently?

Will the husband rise to the role of primary homemaker for the children? He will have to get them up in the morning, see that they have breakfast, and are off to school safely and on time.

How will the decision be made, if for example, both partners have rewarding and challenging careers, but the occasion has now arisen where one has been offered the opportunity, or is being compelled to take a relocation to another city?

When both parents work outside the home, both are likely to arrive home tired at the end of each day. There are still things to be done. Kids to feed and bathe. Laundry and a mountain of housework to be done. Also, the lawn needs cutting. What about dinner for the family?

Wife, when he comes home from work tired mentally and physically, and he doesn't want to talk about what went wrong at work, how are you going to respond?

He's not giving you the old silent treatment. He wants to shift gears, and put the office or shop out of his mind. Don't press him on it.

Husband, when you come home from work tired and irritable and the only living thing she's had to talk to all day has been a cranky two year old, she's going to be expecting some real conversation with you.

All you may want to do is crash in front of the TV, but you will have a happier time of it if you pay her some attention.

Husband, if your wife enjoys career success, and ends up earning more than you earn, give her due credit for her accomplishments. Be careful that jealousy does not get the upper hand in your relationship.

One of the most stressful situations a family may be faced with is the loss of employment by the major breadwinner. The loss of employment brings on a whirlwind of emotion. Self-worth is called into doubt.

***

During my career years, I experienced job loss on several occasions. Typically, the time between layoff and finding a new position was three months each. Once, it was an entire year. I know the frustrations, and the stress of involuntary unemployment.

***

The threat of major financial losses, the loss of home, property, other possessions, and even your standing within your community takes its toll on the emotional, spiritual, and even the physical health of the entire family.

During such times, it is imperative that the family bond remains strong. Wife, if your husband is in this situation, be as supportive as you can. He already feels the world is against him. The last thing he needs is to feel that you are against him as well.

More than likely he found himself in this position through no fault of his own. Now more than ever, your reliance on God to be your Source is vital.

Such times will test your faith. Stay strong in the Word and make sure your prayer life is alive and active. Seek spiritual and emotional support from trusted friends and family if you feel the need to do so.

Those situations often put a strain on the marital relationship. If the wife is not careful, she may withdraw her emotional, and even physical support for him.

She may blame him for the loss of the job and the resulting financial uncertainty. Even though this is an irrational reaction to the situation, it is an emotional one and thus an easy trap for her to fall into.

If she sees him as being inadequate to fulfill his role as breadwinner, she will likely see him as inadequate as a man, and thus undeserving of her love and affection. Wife, I charge you to avoid this at all cost.

Remember the vows you made to him on that first day. Don't violate them. Leaving him emotionally is just as damaging, and just as wrong as leaving him physically.

He has lost enough, and to lose your emotional support on top of all else is not only immensely unfair, it is against God's pattern for the role of a wife in the marriage relationship.

Husband, if your roles are reversed here, the same advice applies to you. Support her with all of your love, and keep her lifted up in prayer.

Never, ever forget that your greatest strength is gained through prayer and your trust in God. This applies to all struggles you are likely to face as a married couple and as a family.

8. Leisure/Recreation

Do you have mutual recreational interests? If not, try to find something fun that you can both enjoy doing together. Allow for time in your busy life to enjoy outside activities.

Don't go overboard though. There is nothing quite so pleasant as quiet time at home, just the two of you. Consider your budget as well.

When children come along, or if the marriage has started with children already present, finding time for fun activities becomes a challenge.

9. Disagreements/Arguments and Differences of Opinions

Reckless words pierce like a sword, but the tongue of the wise brings healing.
(Prov 12:18 NIV)

Learn to fight constructively. Disagreements are certain to arise in any marriage. How you learn to deal with those will go a long way in determining the quality of your relationship.

Learn to guard your tongue. In the heat of the argument, cruel words can be said. Words which would never be said if you took the time to think before speaking.

He who guards his mouth and his tongue keeps himself from calamity. (Prov 21:23 NIV)

That is great advice because you will regret the cruel words. And once spoken they're terribly hard to retract.

Cardinal Rule Number 1: NEVER USE THE "D" WORD! Don't ever sow the seed of that idea. Though you may not seriously want to consider it, and though you may in truth be using it simply as an attempted "wakeup call" to your spouse, once that seed has been planted, it may take root and grow. And like a noxious weed, it is terribly hard to kill.

Even if the point you are trying to get across is valid, heated emotion will make it difficult for your mate to accept that point in the spirit you intended.

There are two extremes you need to avoid.

1. Letting emotion take total control.

2. Avoiding the need to talk it out.

Heated debate may be in order and sometimes the release of emotion is healthy. Good advice is to not keep harboring resentments and ill feelings.

The quicker those can be released, assuming that it's not in an uncontrolled rage, or a rage of any sort, the quicker the problem, real or perceived can be dealt with and the healing process begun.

Do not keep ill feelings hidden inside. They will build up and cause both emotional and physical harm to you. Your mate will suffer as well as he or she will never know what is bothering you, nor why a distance is building between you.

Stress within a relationship, if not overbearing, can help build strength in that relationship. Just like a muscle grows stronger through the strain of exercise, the tensions of disagreements bring with them the realization of why you value each other. It is exercise for your marriage.

Like exercise, when controlled, it causes muscles to grow and strengthen. Too much can cause damage and should be avoided.

> ***If you are angry, don't sin by nursing your grudge. Don't let the sun go down with you still angry-get over it quickly; for when you are angry, you give a mighty foothold to the devil.***
> (Eph 4:26-27 TLB)

The enemy of your soul is also the enemy of your marriage. The advice to never let the sun go down while you are still angry is among the best you can receive.

Don't give your mate the silent treatment. *Never go to bed and turn your face to the wall giving your mate the cold shoulder treatment.*

Your mate may be just as cold in his or her response, but rest assured; down inside he or she is hurting.

Even if you are not the cause of the problem, don't let pride or an unwarranted sense of wounded dignity and personal rights get in the way. Take it upon yourself to make the first move to heal the hurt.

What happens if *both* of you take that first steps to make it right? I don't have to answer that. Kissing and making up is sweet indeed. And a whole lot of fun!

10. Communications

COMMUNICATION (ko-myoo-ni-kay-shon) n.

Female... The open sharing of thoughts and feelings with one's partner.
Male... Leaving a note before taking off on a fishing trip with the boys.

> ***The mouth of the righteous man utters wisdom, and his tongue speaks what is just.***
> (Ps 37:30 NIV)

Husband, talk to your wife. Wife, talk to your husband. Learn to talk to and with each other. Not AT each other. Talk and listen. Learn to pay attention to what the other person is saying.

Real communication is two way. That means, what is said by one is received and understood by the other.

It is easy to tune out the other, and while appearing to listen, not listen at all. Husband, we men are generally poor listeners. Nodding and mumbling, "uh huh" is not listening.

The dangers of failing to communicate are many. For one, the relationship does not grow. You do not get to know each other.

Also, since all humans have an essential need to share hopes, dreams, ideas, and to simply hear the voice of another human, lacking that in a relationship, sometimes leads to a risk of one looking elsewhere for the filling of that need.

Intimate communication outside of marriage is dangerous, and may lead to physical relations outside of marriage. *Husband, heed this warning.*

Do not allow another woman to become your sounding board for problems within your marriage. Wife, you get the same advice from me.

Try to eliminate distractions that hamper good communications. Noises, other conversations going on around you, the television, radio, are just a few of the potential distractions.

You can't talk effectively with your mate if he or she is totally engrossed in a favorite TV program. He or she will not hear half of what you are saying. You will feel like you are competing for his or her attention.

Certainly, you cannot be 100 percent attentive all of the time. And you can't expect your mate to not grow weary if you insist on talk, talk, talk every minute you're in each other's presence. A little quiet time goes a long way.

> **Do not let any unwholesome talk come out of your mouths, but only what is helpful for building others up according to their needs, that it may benefit those who listen.**
> (Eph 4:29-30 NIV)

This ties in very closely with the previous topic on disagreements. What you say to your mate should always be intended to build up. Not tear down. Ask yourself, "is what I want to say to her or him intended to hurt or to help?"

Pay attention to the manner of what you say as well as the content of what you say. Don't say the right thing in a wrong way. That can cause hurt, or at the least, misunderstanding.

11. Respect your mate.

Never, ever, ever publicly criticize him or her. Never make him or her the butt of a joke before anyone else.

It may seem funny at the time, and your mate may even laugh along on the outside, but inside, he or she probably wants to crawl in a hole for embarrassment.

Be careful of ridiculing remarks made to your mate, even in private. They hurt and they're destructive to your relationship. Build him or her up. Don't be constantly putting them down.

Be quick to apologize over improper or hurtful remarks. For that matter, be quick to apologize over any wrong you have done to your mate.

12. Be quick and be generous with your praise for your mate.

Everyone loves to receive the pat on the back. Especially when it comes in a verbal form. We all like to hear words of appreciation.

Of course this need extends outside of marriage as well as inside, but it is especially appreciated when it comes from the one who means the most to you.

"Honey, you did a great job painting that cabinet. It looks wonderful. You're a great man. And I love you."

I know what it means to me when I hear my wife speak words like that to me.

"Or, simply saying, for no particular reason, "you're a great man. I'm proud to be your wife."

I enjoy speaking words of praise to her as well. And I make a practice of doing it often. Typically, every day. At least once every day, and more often that that is the general rule here.

Do I say it too much? Too often? So far, she has not told me to lighten up with the praise.

Tell her she is pretty. Tell her she is beautiful. The two terms don't particularly mean the same thing to a woman. Tell her both. And mean it when you speak the words.

If you're holding her face between your two hands, and looking directly into her eyes while you say those words of praise to her, if she is like most women, she will melt inside.

> ***How beautiful you are, my darling!***
> (Song 1:15 NIV)

> ***How beautiful you are, my darling!***
> ***Oh, how beautiful!*** (Song 4:1 NIV)

Never stop telling her how attractive she is to you. And never stop telling her how pretty she is. There will come a time when looks begin to fade.

Nature and age are not always kind to us. Then it will be all the more important that she hear words of affirmation from you.

Wife, it will not hurt you to tell him words of affirmation as well. Tell him he is handsome. Or for men, simply saying we look great. Or words such as "you're a good-looking man," mean more than you might guess.

Chapter 7 - Additional Thoughts

Allow her freedom. Don't restrict the full potential of her womanhood and her humanness. If she has dreams and aspirations, encourage those and support her in any way you can.

If she chooses to work outside of the home and have a full and meaningful career, let her. Don't be reluctant in your tolerance and encouragement. If she chooses to be a stay-at-home wife and mom, support her in that choice as well.

If she wants to have friends, hobbies, attend classes of some sort, or learn new skills, let her. Encourage her and don't make her feel like you resent the attention taken away from you.

Wife, be sensitive to the fact that your husband still needs your attention. Just as he should balance work and home life, you should balance your work or your outside activities and your home life.

Husband, don't let your freedom to have outside friends and interests (and just like for the wife, we're referring to healthy interests) take priority over your duties and obligations to your wife. She needs your attention too.

Respect each other's differences and needs. Men and women have different temperaments, different likes and different needs. The more you learn about your mate, the better you will be able to understand and tolerate those differences.

Work hard to get to know your mate. Simply living in the close proximity of marriage will teach you a lot about each other, but you have to really work at building the close relationship whereby you really know each other.

This is not unlike our relationship with God. We can know God or we can **KNOW** God. It's a matter of intimacy, and degrees of knowledge. Do you really know everything that makes her glad or sad? Do you as the old phrase goes, know what "makes her tick"?

Don't try to change each other. Perhaps I should have put this as the number one topic on the first page, for it is a matter over which not only relationships may be destroyed, but deep wounds are suffered and it kills spirits.

I may be amiss, but I believe, as I have observed, that more often women will attempt to change their men, than will men try to change their women.

It may be the nurturing gene at work in women, or perhaps they simply have different ideals and expectations than men. It is less common that a husband or boyfriend will suggest or even insist on changes to her style of dress, hairstyle, or makeup preferences. He likes what he sees in her appearance, and is more likely to accept her as she looks.

A man is initially attracted to a woman based on her appearance. Do not think that shallow. It is natural and as God intended. Don't try to change, it or argue against the rightness of it.

If he does not like her appearance, he is not attracted to her and will not seek to pursue her favor. For that reason, it is not common for him to call for major changes on her part. There are exceptions of course. Chances are, she will make greater demands for him to change than he will make of her.

The demands for him to change often go beyond just his choice of clothing styles and how he cuts his hair. They often go to the heart of who he is, for who he is, very much determines what he likes to do.

What a man does with his life, in terms of career choices, and even the hobbies he enjoys, very much follows what he is personality wise. A wife making unreasonable demands can often kill not only his ego and his sense of manhood, but his spirit as well.

I have known individual men who gave in to the demands of a new bride to give up his dream of a career, which to her was undesirable for one reason or other.

For her, he chose something else, and remained an unhappy shell for the remainder of his life. Forever filled with regret over what he missed and what he could have become. What he greatly desired to become and make of himself, he never did or became.

Wife, if he is a soldier, and you make him give that life up to become an accountant, or even a doctor or lawyer, you will no longer have the man you fell in love with.

If he has a lifelong dream to enter law enforcement, or the military, or take on any other career that you may see as overly risky, if that desire is more than just a passing fancy on his part, you do yourself and him a great disservice if you compel him to give up that dream.

The greater damage is done to him, but it will reflect in your marriage relationship as well.

If he likes to ride motorcycles, or likes to own firearms, get over your fear of those things. Yes, there is reason for and the responsibility to exercise proper precautions.

But if he is exercising due respect for these hobbies, and not reckless in his enjoyment of them, let him enjoy them. If you cannot learn to like them yourself, at least allow him to enjoy them. And don't hound him about it.

Do not exhibit signals of shame toward him. If he has a tattoo when you meet and begin your relationship, for instance, and you do not like tattoos, do not, even in jest, put your hand or other covering over his tattoo attempting to hide it from view in the company of others, as though it is something you are ashamed of. I once saw a wife do that.

You are sending the signal that you are ashamed of him. If he does not have one, and he expresses the desire to you to gain one, then you two have room for discussion. Of course you have every right to voice your approval or disapproval over the matter.

Husband, your body is not your own. If it is a whim or an impulse on your part, you owe her the respect of valuing her opinions.

There is a saying I've seen on social media recently. It says, "unless he's wearing a diaper, you're not going to change him."

That is very good advice, and all women should take note. The outlaw, or bad boy may come on as enticing to you, but the only one changed in a relationship with this sort of man will be you. And it won't be for the better.

Guys, be careful that you do not try to change her in ways which will make her less than the person she is.

Although it is not as common today, I have known of families where the practice is for the men, once married, to turn their wives into what might amount to slaves.

Take away their career dreams, take away their driver's license (yes, I've seen that happen) and turn them into what amounts to docile domestics. The old saying is "keep them barefoot and pregnant.

If that's your family culture, break it. Ladies, if the man you are contemplating marrying is of that family culture, you have a choice to make. But make it before you walk down the aisle.

Deal with the little irritants and quirks you so dislike *now*. If those annoying little habits or personality quirks bother you now, how much more so will they irritate you after just a few years of marriage?

Are they things that can or should be changed? Have you talked to him or her about them? Are they worth bothering with? Will you get used to them and completely overlook them in good time?

It really is *not* important how the toilet paper roll is oriented on the roller. Likewise the paper towel roll in the kitchen. *Whether it feeds over the top, or from underneath matters not a hill of beans.* It is not a matter to argue over.

I know that is a controversial position on my part, but really, are there not more important things to discuss and disagree on between you?

The same thing applies to the toothpaste tube. Eventually it all gets used up whether it is squeezed from the bottom, the top or even the middle. It's not worth having heated arguments over.

Are your mate's quirks any worse than the quirks that *you* have?

Share each other's dreams. If we're alive and have any degree of passion for anything, we will have hopes and dreams. Those may be simple, or they may be grandiose. A young person dreams of adulthood, a career, getting married, raising children, and being happy.

A young man may have a dream of earning a degree in political science, entering public service, and eventually running for high public office. Perhaps even the presidency.

When we have a dream, by the very definition, a dream is a passion. A passion burns so deeply inside us that we usually cannot keep it quiet. Who better to tell than the one you love the most?

You may think the dream is totally outlandish or at the least unattainable. You may be right. Be careful. You might be wrong.

How tragic it would be to discourage someone you care deeply about from pursuing his or her dream that though you thought it was unattainable, in truth could have been realized?

Someone I know recently told me that throughout her life she had developed some "good ideas" but others told her they were really bad ideas.

They sounded realistic and achievable when she described them to me. She had been discouraged from trying to realize those dreams. What a shame. She never even bothered to try. Why should she?

Tell each other your dreams. Share your dreams with your mate. Make your dreams your mate's dreams, and make your mate's dreams your dreams. Become involved at least, in the sense of appreciation and support.

Build dreams around your marriage. Look with high hopes to the future. No, we do not know what the future holds for us, and Scripture tells us that we have no assurance of tomorrow, but we should still plan as though we will have many years to share with each other.

If you are just starting your marriage early in your adult years, you have your entire lives ahead of you as clean and unwritten as a fresh un-painted canvas.

You will begin and raise a family. You will begin careers. At least one of you will. You may buy a house. You will plan summer vacation trips. You will enjoy watching your children grow and eventually turn into adults themselves. You will see them marry and begin families of their own.

All this is assuming that God allows you the years and the health to enjoy these things.

Even if you come together in a marriage that is not your first, and perhaps you already have achieved some of these dreams, you will begin your own set of dreams, hopes and aspirations.

Deal with jealousy. Do not be jealous of your mate. The most common form of jealousy is the fear of losing the affections of your mate to another. There is another form of jealousy that is just as destructive to the marriage relationship. That is the jealousy of your mate's success, his or her friends, family, or anything "good" in his or her life.

> *Anger is cruel and fury overwhelming, but who can stand before jealousy?* (Prov 27:4 NIV)

The problem with such jealousy has been dealt with in previous topics such as your mate's friends, or family. Jealousy will cause harm not only to your mate, but to you as well.

Jealousy is one of the most destructive of human emotions. It will also cause sour relationships beyond just yours with your mate. Family and friends are affected as well.

Talk to your mate about those things which you struggle with such as jealousy. Examine the causes if you can identify them. Most of all make the problem a matter of prayer. In severe cases, godly counsel is probably advisable.

Don't be so possessive of his or her time that you can never allow for outside activities on his or her part, nor allow them to spend a little time with a friend or family member.

Without Trust, the marriage is in grave danger of failing. Trust is more than simply not fearing wrong doing on the part of your mate.

Certainly, that's what we expect from our marriage partner. Fidelity. Words in the wedding vows say "forsaking all others." Or something in similar language meaning the same thing.

But trust also means, "having confidence in." He trusts her to fulfil the roles she promised to fulfil. And she trusts him to fulfil the roles he promised to fulfil.

He trusts her to manage the home front - assuming that she is not working outside the home. And she trusts him to be the provider and protector. The "breadwinner" if that is the order of the careers between them.

But it goes a little deeper, and here is where the word "confidence" fits as a meaning for trust.

Let's say, the washing machine suddenly develops a leak. Granted, not all men are skilled or handy at being fixers. If he is not, then he's not likely to object to your calling a service rep from the appliance repair shop.

But if he is. Or is at least halfway handy at such things, and he sets out to make the repairs himself, it won't do his ego any good if you criticize and belittle his ability to successfully complete the task.

In other words, if you do not trust him, or have confidence in him, chances are, he's not going to offer to fix many things around the house that may need fixing.

If you're looking over his shoulder all the while he is working, and making little comments alluding to your fear that he is going to mess up the job rather than fix the problem, you're showing that he is not worthy of your trust.

Husbands, the same applies for you. If she is managing the household finances, are you going to trust her, and not constantly be afraid that she is going to mess up and leave you on the verge of bankruptcy? Or perhaps not something so dramatic. But still. Trust her. Trust her just as you expect her to trust you.

***

We once rode in the car of another couple. I don't remember where we were going that evening, but as often happens when people go to an event, they may share the ride. We rode along with them.

Throughout the entire drive, to and from the destination, the wife filled the role of the proverbial backseat driver from Hell. Of course she was not sitting in the back seat.

Nothing he did as far as driving was right. She seemed to be perpetually terrified that he was going to get us all killed.

She was convinced, or so it seemed, that he had to be the worst driver to ever hold a driver's license.

Coming and going, he never made any driving blunders. He never made a dangerous driving move. There was nothing wrong with his driving.

She simply did not trust him. She was convinced that at any moment, he would make a wrong turn, probably in front of oncoming traffic. Or he would run a redlight and be hit by another car. Or he would lose control and the car would roll over.

I have often wondered in what other area of their married life did she not trust him. I felt badly for him.

***

A quarrelsome wife is like a constant dripping on a rainy day; restraining her is like restraining the wind or grasping oil with the hand. (Prov 27:15-16 NIV)

Husband, don't be that way with your wife. Learn to trust her. Learn to have confidence in whatever she sets out to do. And support her with praise and complements.

Brag on her before others. Let the world know that she is special. And talented, and smart, and beautiful.

Avoid Hyperbole and List building. I once knew of a wife who, having seen her husband miss a few street turns when he should have known where he was driving, for he did usually know the way, chide him with "you never know where you're going."

"Never?" Did he make wrong turns everywhere he went enroute to their desired direction? Of course not. But sometimes missing a turn, as we can all do now and then, particularly if something distracts us, sometimes becomes always. Or so she accused him of doing.

It amounts to her saying, "you never do the right thing when it comes to getting us to our desired destination."

Now I am sure husbands can do the same thing. "You always burn the chicken when you cook it." Well, does she always, or did she simply burn it one time?

We can do damage to our marriage partner's self-confidence and we can make him or her feel little and inadequate in their own eyes when we constantly tell them they are doing it wrong. Whatever the "it" is.

Usually, such treatment comes with the lack of ever telling them how good they do things. After a while, nothing they do is ever done right, even in their own mind.

List building is similar, and it often contains a large dose of hyperbole. We all make mistakes. I remember how badly I messed up certain things in my early marriage years. It seems that the younger we are, the more prone we are to mess things up.

A list builder, remembers a mistake you made in the past. Sometimes that mistake may have been made years ago. But in any argument, you will be reminded of your mistake.

And, being a builder of lists, it usually will not be only one thing. There will be a list of things you have done wrong. And because of hyperbole, you will learn that you have always repeated that same mistake.

"You always leave the car gas tank empty, just when I'm in a hurry to drive the kids to school." Meaning in essence, one time, or maybe it has happened more than once, he forgot to fill up the tank when it was low, and she was late getting the kids to school because she had to stop and fill it up first.

But with the list builder and hyperbole, it must happen one hundred percent of the time. Perhaps the last time he did forget was four years ago. It matters not. It's an always failure on his part.

Husband, she doesn't always burn the toast. Perhaps she did a time or two, or even a few times. That's not the same as "always."

> ***"I, yes, I alone am he who blots away your sins for my own sake and will never think of them again."*** (Isa 43:25-26 TLB)

If God wipes out our sins, and even our past mistakes and shortcomings, how much more should we wipe out, even the memory of the failures of our spouse?

From the Author

Throughout this book I have stressed the value of Christ based counseling. There are times when in spite of our best efforts to solve problems within our marriage relationship, we are unable to arrive at suitable answers or solutions.

Prayer, study of the Word of God, and talking it out with each other will resolve a multitude of problems within a marriage. But they may need more.

Don't be afraid to call on others who are willing and able to offer support, advice and prayerful counsel. Be certain though that those you call on for such help are themselves firm in their own faith, and responsible, and that their lives and teachings align squarely with the Word of God.

Some matters should be handled only by those who have prepared themselves professionally. Speak to your pastor, your singles pastor, or other trusted minister. Let them help you determine what level of counseling assistance you need.

Pastor, be very sensitive to the needs of the young married or soon to be married couple who is coming to you for advice and counsel on their marriage.

Be sure that you are qualified and feel comfortable before committing to help them deal with the problem or problems they are facing.

Don't be quick to want to possess the problem if it is something you know would be beyond your own training, knowledge, or experience level.

Or, if you feel that you may be too close to the situation, or to the lives of the couple, or to one of the parties to be as objective as you should be. Or if it concerns an area you are uncomfortable dealing with.

There is no shame in admitting that the situation they are going through is beyond your ability or experience to help them with.

Be prepared to offer prayerful support, but also to refer them to professional or more experienced resources when it is applicable.

In all cases, whether you are handling the counseling or not, treat the couple with respect, and afford them their due dignity and confidentiality. Pray for them. Pray with them. Keep all things confidential. Be professional in dealing with tender hearts.

About the Author

Dan lives with his wife Patsy in Paragould, Arkansas. Dan and Patsy were both widowed, and they came to meet each other through a local widows and widowers connection group. They very soon knew that they were meant to be a couple together, and they were married within a few months of their meeting.

Dan and Patsy are certified marriage mentors. And with a combined total of almost one hundred years of marriage between them, they have, what they hope is a thing or two to offer couples at all stages of married life.

Both of them have counseling experience, and though not certified marriage counselors, and do not engage in the practice professionally, they have worked with couples experiencing marital troubles as part of what they believe is their calling as a service and ministry.

They are active in church work. Their home church in Paragould focuses on addiction recovery, and both of them serve in different capacities within that ministry.

Dan currently teaches a men's Bible study class for one of the men's addiction recovery groups

Dan has also published several novels and this is his first non-fiction work to publish.

Other Titles by the Author

Books in the Legacy of Abigail series

A Ship Called Abigail
Voyage of Abigail
When Love Finds Hannah
An Empty Quiet Place

Other books by Dan W. Dooley

Mister Weatherspoon's Unfortunate Clock
Miss Penny's Wedding Dress